PARTICIPATING SPONSORS

THE TCI COMPANIES

Kodak

Nikon®
We take the world's
greatest pictures.®

I

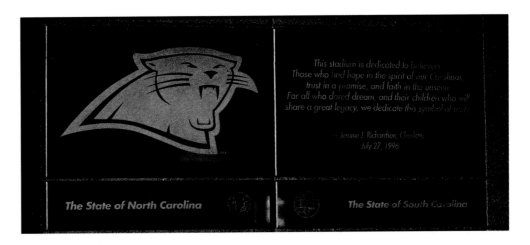

This stadium is dedicated to believers.
Those who had hope in the spirit of our Carolinas,
trust in a promise, and faith in the unseen.
For all who dared dream, and their children who will
share a great legacy, we dedicate this symbol of unity.

— Jerome J. Richardson, Charlotte
July 27, 1996

The State of North Carolina   The State of South Carolina

Miracle on Mint Street

Not all of the thousands who streamed into the great stadium on Sunday morning, September 1, 1996, were wide-eyed with excitement. I, for one, could hardly speak. And I had a hunch—later confirmed—that Jerry Richardson felt the same way.

How could we possibly have pulled this off? How could we be here, eight years and nine months since Jerry almost quietly told a media gathering on the mezzanine level of the Radisson Hotel that he would seek an NFL team for the Carolinas and privately build a stadium to house it? History says the longer the dream drags on, the slimmer the chance, when it comes to landing trophy franchises. Yet here we were, 3,190 days (as Atlanta counted down the Olympics) since Richardson's hopeful proclamation, and we not only had the franchise, we had a building ready for its first official home game that had been called "the finest football stadium ever built" by the commissioner of the NFL and owners from Pittsburgh to San Francisco.

"Teamwork and harmony. We believe in teamwork and harmony," Jerry Richardson would say. How many times we heard that over those 3,000-odd days? Today, September 1, 1996, it was clear who the "team" in "teamwork" was. The "team"—the greater team who also would be heroes today—poured through the 80-foot black granite entry portals, between the 20-foot long panther statues and into the seats which nearly 60,000 of them had taken control of with Permanent Seat Licenses. No wonder that Richardson, as the first act of his first 15 minutes as an officially anointed NFL franchise owner, had taken the microphone from Commissioner Paul Tagliabue on that happy day in Chicago and said, "I want to speak to all of those (at the time) 50,000 PSL holders back in the Carolinas. You made this possible, and when we get back home, we're gonna say thank you, thank you, thank you!" But this bright Sunday morning, far more than just PSL holders were exultant in the dream come true. Thousands who had bought single game tickets, hundreds of media from throughout the Carolinas and hundreds of thousands of others who would enjoy this day on television and over the radio also realized that this was the day that the Miracle on Mint Street had at last come to pass.

Walking up the ramp with my wife that morning, I looked out across the city and thanked God that it had somehow happened, that so many crises had been overcome. I reflected on the incredible patience, resilience and determination of Jerry and Mark Richardson and their family, who could have had no idea of the magnitude of length of the struggle ahead when they decided to try. What did the national oddsmaker who rated our chances as a 50-1 longshot think now?

The day would unfold, as this book so beautifully details, like classic poetry. So much was required of so many to get us to this day that surely the Panthers would cap it with a win, and they did. Some would say that such victories—the Panthers were 3-point underdogs—are too much to expect. But in this house, all things are possible. That is its legacy and surely its future. And on September 1, 1996, it was a lesson of that "Day to Remember."

—Max Muhleman

Kodak Professional Films were used throughout
Carolina Panthers Sunday, primarily Kodak
EKTACHROME Professional E100SW film.

Photographers used the new Nikon F5 as the
primary camera for *Carolina Panthers Sunday*.

Pachyderm Press

Copyright ©1996.
Pachyderm Press, Birmingham, Alabama.
First published in 1996. All rights reserved.
No part of this book may be reproduced
by any means without the written permission
of the publisher.
Printed in the United States of America.
ISBN 0-9639505-1-7

CAROLINA PANTHERS SUNDAY

Editor
WALLACE SEARS
Supervising Photographer
JOE MᶜNALLY
Assistant Supervising Photographer
BEN VAN HOOK
Project Sponsorship & Marketing
THE TCI COMPANIES
LINDA HIGGISON, President

Photographers: **ANNIE GRIFFITHS BELT, NICOLE BENGIVENO, JIM GENSHEIMER, LYNN JOHNSON, ART MERIPOL, RICK RICKMAN, DAVID ROARK, JOEL SARTORE, SCOTT WISEMAN**
Carolina Panthers Team Photographer: **SCOTT CUNNINGHAM**
Richardson Family Photographer: **LES DUGGINS**
The TCI Companies, Team Concepts International: **RON PETERSON, DIRECTOR**
Shoot Producer: **NINA SABO**
Chief Photography Assistant: **MARK ASHMAN**
Administrative Manager: **LAREE BROWN**
Facilities & Equipment Manager: **JERRY BROWN**
Coordinators: **CHRISTINA FETTERS, CECE WILCK**
Book Design: **BEN BURFORD**
Print Coordinator: **GLENN PETRY**

Photographer
BEN VAN HOOK

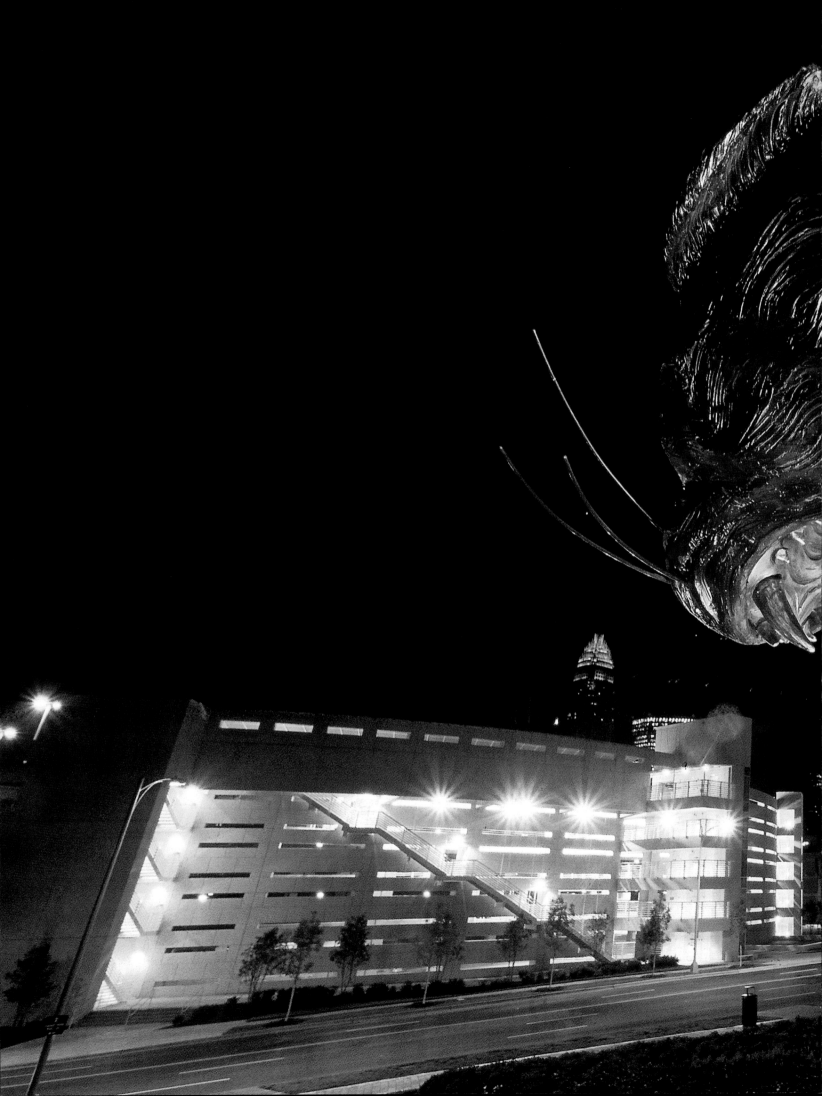

RICK RICKMAN

NICOLE BENGIVENO

EARLY MORNING

Dawn breaks over the Carolinas. Fans young and old have waited years
for this day to arrive. And it arrives gloriously. This is the day that the
Carolina Panthers play their first regular-season game in
Ericsson Stadium. There is pride involved in this day. Pride of a family,
pride of a city and region, pride of the fans, pride of a team and
organization and pride of the tens-of-thousands of others who will help
make this day a success. Throughout the region, people prepare for this
memorable occasion. But even as people in the city and surrounding
area slowly wake this Sunday, others at Ericsson Stadium have already
been hard at work for hours. They have been waiting for this event,
too. As the sun slowly glows brighter in the eastern Carolina skies
it illuminates a new day and the beginning of a new era
born out of hopes and dreams and teamwork.

Photographer
JOE McNALLY

FOLLOWING PAGES
Photographer
JOEL SARTORE

Ericsson Stadium is lit against the early morning
sunrise, ready for the first regular-season NFL
game in Charlotte.

Photographer
DAVID ROARK

Across the city, people slowly awake and
prepare for the day ahead.
Photographer
JOEL SARTORE

Final inspections are made throughout
the stadium prior to opening the gates.

Photographer

ANNIE GRIFFITHS BELT

Coach Dom Capers, Jerry Richardson and
Mark Richardson join the team at the hotel
for breakfast.

Photographer
MARK ASHMAN

PRE GAME

Excitement builds. Across the region, fans make their way to uptown Charlotte full of anticipation. Friends meet in pre-arranged locations to view the game on television or to listen to the radio broadcast. Fathers and sons and mothers and daughters all gather together dressed in blue and black and silver as food is prepared and set out on kitchen tables or at tailgating locations. At the stadium, everyone from players to coaches to management to vendors have now arrived and are in the midst of game preparations. Warm-ups take place. Equipment is checked. Costumes and uniforms are fitted just so. Everyone focuses on the moment when Carolinas history will be made — when the Panthers take the field.

Photographer
RICK RICKMAN

FOLLOWING PAGES
Photographer
NICOLE BENGIVENO

The mid-morning sun brightens up the landscape
surrounding Ericsson Stadium.

Photographer
NICOLE BENGIVENO

Crews begin to unload and arrange the thousands of traffic cones used to direct pedestrians and vehicles safely throughout Charlotte.

Photographer
JOEL SARTORE

ABOVE

James Worthington of Cincinnati, Ohio, blows up his game-day souvenir Panther helmet.

Photographer
JOEL SARTORE

RIGHT

Radio personalities John Boy and Billy are among the thousands of Carolina fans who couldn't wait for the first game, and tried to make the day last as long as possible.

Photographer
LES DUGGINS

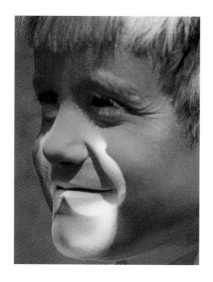
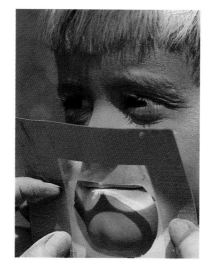

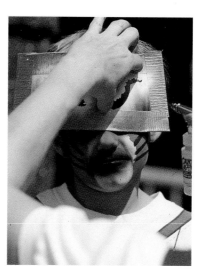

ABOVE
Heidi Gitts joins thousands of other fans
in the popular practice of having her
face painted at a booth outside
the stadium.
Photographer
ART MERIPOL

ABOVE
Heidi Gitts joins thousands of other fans
in the popular practice of having her
face painted at a booth outside
the stadium.
Photographer
ART MERIPOL

OPPOSITE PAGE
Maria Adriano sees the results of her
make-up under the watchful eye of
one of the team's namesakes.
Photographer
ART MERIPOL

John Schiel of Weddington, North Carolina,
cooks up snacks before the game.

Photographer
DAVID ROARK

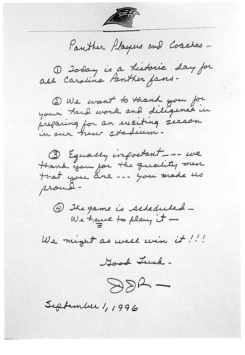

Panther Players and Coaches —

① Today is a historic day for all Carolina Panther fans.

② We want to thank you for your hard work and diligence in preparing for an exciting season in our new stadium.

③ Equally important — — we thank you for the quality men that you are — — you make us proud.

④ The game is scheduled — We have to play it —

We might as well win it !!!

Good Luck —

September 1, 1996

With make-up finished and costumes on,
the Top Cats prepare to take their place
on the field.

Photographer
NINA SABO

BOTTOM
Ron Pitts has final make-up applied for the
regional telecast of the game on
Fox Network Sports.

Photographer
ART MERIPOL

Young Jonathan Vaughn of Charlotte, watches
the pre-game network broadcast. He is
among the millions of Carolina Panthers
fans who could hardly wait for the
kick-off of the first regular season
game in Charlotte.

Photographer
NICOLE BENGIVENO

FIRST GAME

NFL Referee Johnny Grier blows his whistle and the teams move forward as Atlanta kicks off. The game is underway. The Panthers win the coin toss, and are also determined to win this game, the first game in their new home. It is an afternoon filled with the greatness of the National Football League. It is filled with spectacular individual performances, and precisely executed team play. The Panther offense mixes a powerful running game with an accurate passing attack. The fans cheer. The defense does not allow a touchdown to be scored. The fans cheer more. Special teams turn in an outstanding performance. Throughout the afternoon the cheering does not stop. It is a grand and glorious day for the Carolina Panthers. This team is supposed to be an underdog but they control both sides of the ball. The final score says it all. 29-6. And the fans cheer on.

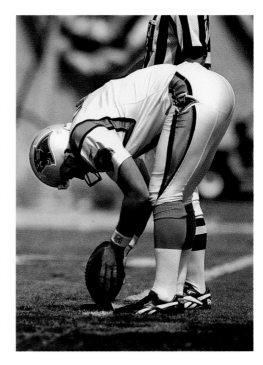

Photographer
BEN VAN HOOK

FOLLOWING PAGES
Photographer
JOE McNALLY

Quarterback Kerry Collins hands off to
Tshimanga Biakabutuka while fullback
Howard Griffith prepares to block.
Photographer
JIM GENSHEIMER

Tshimanga Biakabutuka makes his
regular season debut as a rookie.
Photographer
SCOTT WISEMAN

Mark Carrier scores the first regular season
touchdown in Ericsson Stadium, catching
a 12-yard pass from Kerry Collins, and
capping a 9-play 64-yard drive on the
Panthers' first possession of the game.

Photographer
BILL WIPPERT

Defensive star Sam Mills keeps an eye on
the Falcon offense.

Photographer
RICK RICKMAN

The Carolina Panthers special teams at work.

Photographer
SCOTT WISEMAN

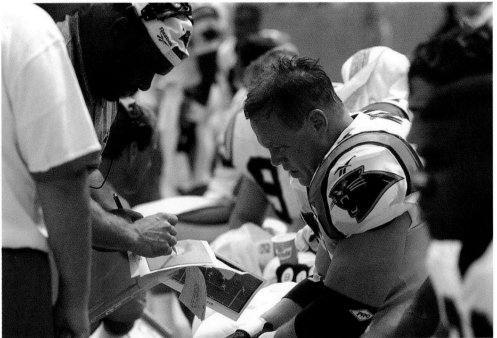

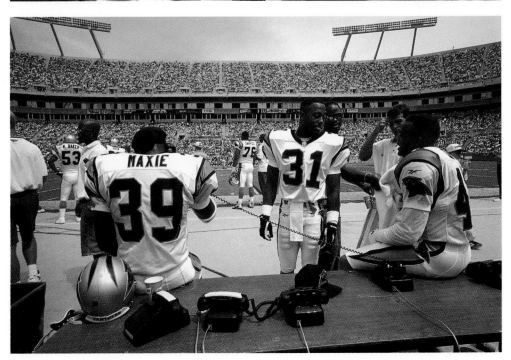

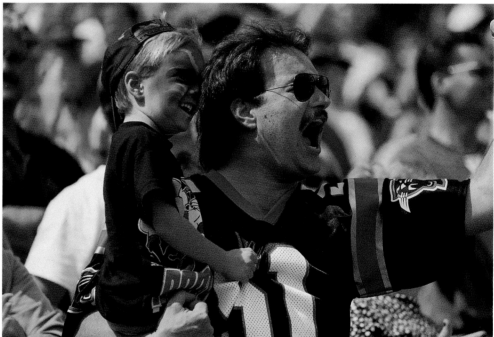

TOP
Dancing for joy is something that comes easy to Patrick Dye on this memorable day, while Kevin Burns watches.

Photographer
LYNN JOHNSON

MIDDLE
Nicholas Scott Cramer hangs on to Dad's jersey, while the two of them cheer the Panthers on.

Photographer
ANNIE GRIFFITHS BELT

BOTTOM
NFL football crosses gender.

Photographer
LYNN JOHNSON

OPPOSITE PAGE
The fans' favorite — Sir Purr!

Photographer
RICK RICKMAN

Drum Major Torrance Lacewell of
Wilmington leads South Carolina
State University during half-time.

Photographer
JOE McNALLY

Cornerback Steve Lofton and the Panther
secondary make things difficult for the
Falcons' receivers.

Photographer
RICK RICKMAN

Meanwhile, the Panther offense makes
spectacular catches.

Photographer
JIM GENSHEIMER

Teamwork pays off with a big win.

Photographer
BEN VAN HOOK

Tackle Mark Dennis checks out the action
on the field during a rest on the sidelines.
Photographer
BEN VAN HOOK

Linebacker Sam Mills keeps the Falcons
in check all afternoon, leading the team
with nine tackles and one assist for the game.

Photographer
RICK RICKMAN

On this day the numbers are clearly
in the Panthers' favor.

Photographer
JIM GENSHEIMER

ABOVE
As the game draws to a close, the fans
cheer the Panthers' victory.

Photographer
ANNIE GRIFFITHS BELT

FOLLOWING PAGES
Linebacker Kevin Greene and Ericsson Stadium
fans celebrate the 29-6 victory.

Photographer
BEN VAN HOOK

THE FAMILY

Photographs by
LYNN JOHNSON

THE TOP CAT

Photographs by
NINA SABO

THE BAND

Photographs by
ANNIE GRIFFITHS BELT

The Charlotte Observer

GameDay

SUNDAY, SEPT. 1, 1996 · Section **G**

Panthers posters

Quarterback Kerry Collins is the first in a series of 10 full-color posters that will profile the Panthers this season. **Page 8G**

Greene ends a tradition

Panthers l Greene will not co of meeting with his kickoff. He says much e

ON SALE TODAY OUTSIDE ERICSS
CHARLOTTE AND BY MAIL, CALL 358-5000 TO W

On sale today: Special keepsake edition, looking back at the '95 season and other highlights

TOM SORENSEN

Starting today, Panthers finally get down for real

Today is a huge day for Charlotte and the Carolinas. N.C. is the Sunshine Band will leave town and the longest pre-season in the history of sports will end.

"What we've got is good ingredients, but the cake is still in the oven and the dough is just beginning to rise."

BILL POLIAN
PANTHERS GENERAL MANAGER, TALKING ABOUT HIS NEW OFFENSE.

Reason to smile

Panthers add horsepower to promising young offense

Justin Thigpen, 12, and brother Nicholas, 10,
browse the newspaper's sports section while
eating breakfast, gathering information
about the day's upcoming game.

ABOVE
After breakfast, the Thigpen family
attends morning worship services at
Christ Episcopal Church on Providence Road.

With the service over, Nicholas is
"ready for some football."

TOP
Richard and son Nicholas prepare hamburger patties for tailgating.

MIDDLE
The family arrives at Ericsson Stadium early enough to enjoy all the pre-game festivities.

BOTTOM
In their seats in the west end-zone, Richard and son Christopher (left) enjoy a perfect Panther afternoon.

At home after the game, Richard and
son Nicholas play touch football.

Youngsters gather at the Thigpen house, and the
father-and-son game soon becomes a
fun-filled neighborhood event.

111

Top Cat Allison Hustad wakes early this Sunday
morning, as does 5-year-old daughter Lauren.

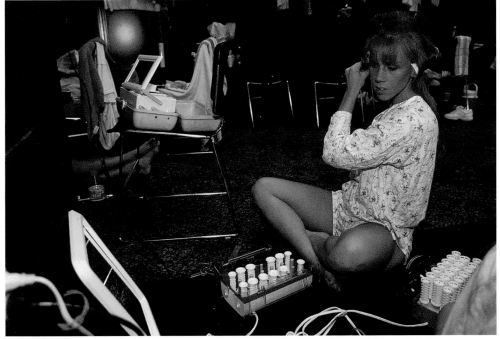

TOP
A pre-dawn paper route is part of Allison's
daily routine, even on game days.

BOTTOM
After warming up and a short rehearsal session
at the Panthers' practice field, Allison prepares
her make-up in the Top Cats' locker room.

TOP
Teamwork among the Top Cats includes
assisting each other with costume adjustments
prior to taking the field.

BOTTOM
Allison helps lead the cheers after a
Panthers score.

114

A bedtime story with Lauren ends Allison's day.

TOP
Rencel Jones of North Carolina A & T cleans his spats at 7 a.m., preparing for the band's half-time performance in Charlotte.

BOTTOM
A "Spirit Session" takes place at the band room prior to leaving for the bus trip to the stadium.

Drum Major Anthony Criss has his head shaved,
an A & T tradition prior to the game.

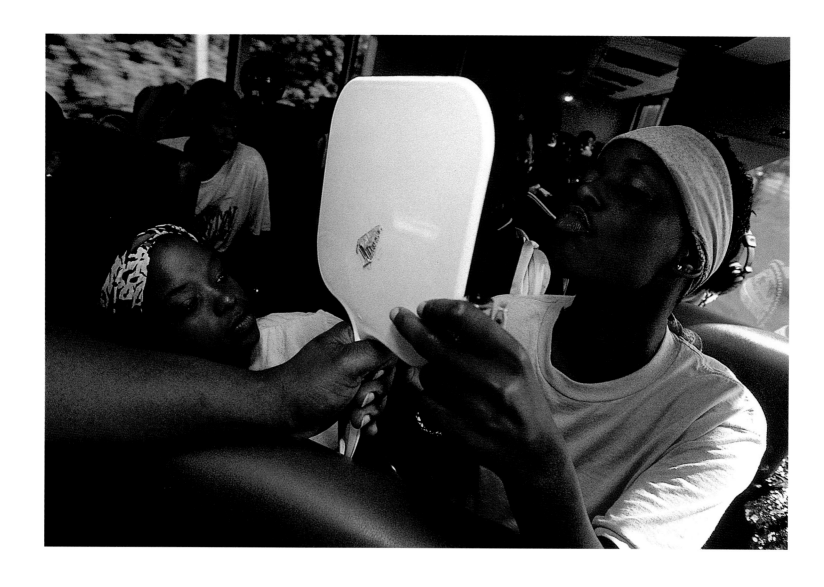

Tanika Dean and Jamila Murray, both of
Greensboro, apply their make-up during
the two-hour bus ride from Greensboro
to the game.

DAY'S END

The celebration begins. Congratulations are in order for the team, coaches and organization, as well as the entire Carolinas. Prayers are given. *It is* a memorable day. The fans remain inside the stadium as long as possible, then finally leave — happy, still cheering for the Panthers. Players give post-game interviews, and express appreciation to their teammates for hard work that produced the win. Fans who attended the game, and others who were part of the television or radio audience all begin to gather at their tailgate vehicles, restaurants, lounges, hotels, homes and apartments for victory parties. Reporters write and videotape their news summaries and commentaries on the game. Equipment managers and stadium workers finalize their duties, while stadium clean-up begins almost immediately. Throughout it all, people are smiling. Smiling for joy. As daylight fades from the sky, the quietness of the night gives many pause to reflect on a magnificent day. Dreams can come true. They did in the Carolinas on September 1, 1996.

Photographer
NICOLE BENGIVENO

FOLLOWING PAGES
Photographer
JOEL SARTORE

Coach Dom Capers greets the players as they
enter the locker room, and congratulates them
for a well-played game.

Photographer
SCOTT CUNNINGHAM

TOP

Fans continue the celebration for the
first victory as they exit
Ericsson Stadium.

Photographer

JOEL SARTORE

BOTTOM

TV crews do wrap-up reports from the field
inside the now-empty stadium.

Photographer

JIM GENSHEIMER

OPPOSITE PAGE

Columnist Furman Bisher, of the
Atlanta Journal & Constitution, ponders the
day's events as Dom Capers' interview room
comments are played over closed-circuit
TV in the Press Box.

Photographer

ART MERIPOL

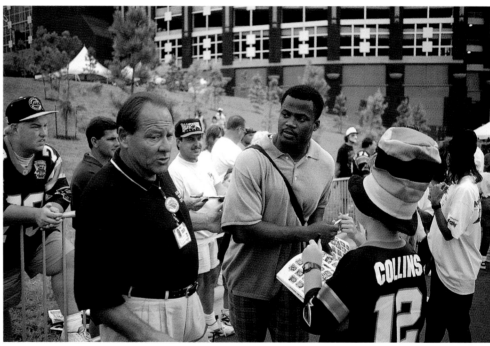

Getting a player's autograph adds to a
youngster's memorable day.

Photographer
BEN VAN HOOK

Tshimanga Biakabutuka pauses to sign
a program for a fan as he departs
the stadium.

Photographer
BEN VAN HOOK

Charlotte Police Officers congratulate
Jerry Richardson on the game's outcome
as he and his wife Rosalind leave.

Photographer
SCOTT WISEMAN

ABOVE
While he may have been delighted by the
final score, young Collin Reaves doesn't
seem too happy to have the day end.

Photographer
JOEL SARTORE

FOLLOWING PAGES
Stadium clean-up begins almost immediately,
preparing for the next event.

Photographer
RICK RICKMAN

Jason Burger and Jennifer Graham celebrate
the Panthers' win with a kiss.

Photographer
JIM GENSHEIMER

Linda Kiss and Skip Ebling high-five
at a post-game celebration.
Photographer
JIM GENSHEIMER

Fans from across the Carolinas stop by the
Dairy Queen for a quick snack as they
leave Charlotte.
Photographer
BEN VAN HOOK

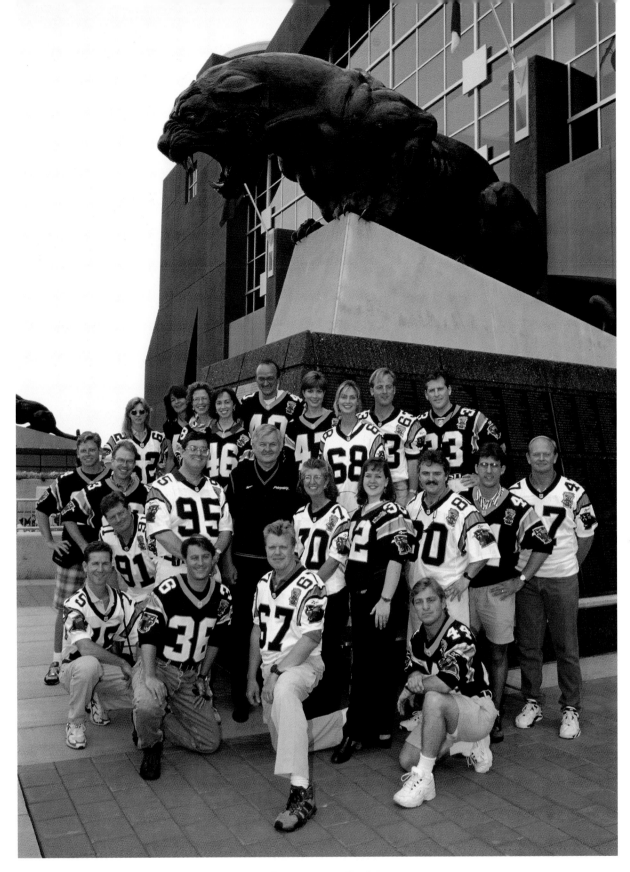

THE STAFF

(Front row kneeling): DAVID ROARK, BEN VAN HOOK (Assistant Supervising Photographer), JOE McNALLY (Supervising Photographer), LES DUGGINS. *(Second row):* MARK ASHMAN, ART MERIPOL, JOEL SARTORE, WALLACE SEARS (Editor/Publisher), JERRY RICHARDSON, LINDA HIGGISON (President, The TCI Companies), LAREE BROWN, SCOTT CUNNINGHAM, JIM GENSHEIMER, JERRY BROWN. *(Third row):* LYNN JOHNSON, NICOLE BENGIVENO, ANNIE GRIFFITHS BELT, NINA SABO, RICK RICKMAN, CECE WILCK, CHRISTINA FETTERS, SCOTT WISEMAN, RON PETERSON.

Photographer
FRED SISSON

EDITOR/PUBLISHER
WALLACE SEARS

Wallace is the founder and Publisher of Pachyderm Press. He was the driving force behind the 1993 publication of *Bryant-Denny Saturday*, the first-ever picture-book published on University of Alabama football. *Bryant-Denny Saturday* reached ninth on the Top 10 non-fiction best seller list for the state of Alabama that year. Wallace spent 8 years in broadcasting in Alabama, writing, reporting and anchoring newscasts at WSFA-TV, Montgomery. With Walt Disney World for 16 years, his last position was Managing Photo Editor for the News & Media Information Department in the Marketing Division, supervising editorial news photo coverage and working with visiting photographers and writers. His work at Walt Disney World provided photographers with shots that were featured on the cover of *Time, Newsweek, Southern Living, TV Guide* and hundreds of newspaper Travel Sections. He has written articles that have appeared in *The Christian Science Monitor, Ideals* magazine, *Alabama* magazine and *Southern Outdoors* magazine.

SUPERVISING PHOTOGRAPHER
JOE McNALLY

Joe is currently working as a staff photographer for *Life* magazine. This appointment took place in fall of 1994 and marked the hiring of the magazine's first staff photographer in more than 20 years.

He started his career in 1976 as a copyboy at the *New York Daily News.* He spent most of the late 1970s shooting for clients such as *The New York Times,* Associated Press and UPI. For two years, he worked as the network still photographer for ABC Television, covering news and sports.

McNally left ABC in 1981 to begin freelancing for magazines. He began working for *Life* in 1984, and was listed on the masthead as a contributing photographer. He was a contract photographer for *Sports Illustrated* for six years, and has shot cover stories for *National Geographic, Life, Time, Newsweek, Sports Illustrated, Fortune* and *New York Magazine.* Joe received a Page One Award from the Newspaper Guild of New York in 1986. He has also placed numerous times in the Pictures of the Year contest, winning first place in magazine illustration in 1988, and first place in magazine product illustration in 1993. In 1996, Joe was awarded third prize for People in the News by The World Press Photo Foundation.

He has taught at the Eddie Adams Workshop for eight years and has lectured on the NPPA Flying Short Course and the *National Geographic* Masters of Contemporary Photography Series. He has worked on numerous "Day in the Life" projects and was a featured exhibitor at the 1991 Festival of Photojournalism in Perpignan, France.

Joe was described by *American Photo* as "perhaps the most versatile photojournalist working today." The magazine listed him in the 1993 edition of the 100 most important people in photography. Joe was the Supervising Photographer for Pachyderm Press' first book, *Bryant-Denny Saturday.* He resides in Westchester, New York, and is married to Michele McNally. They have two daughters, Caitlin, 11, and Claire, 4.

ASSISTANT SUPERVISING
PHOTOGRAPHER - BEN VAN HOOK

Ben is a contract photographer with Black Star and Duomo Photo Agency, both in New York. He shares the 1989 Pulitzer Prize with other members of the staff of the *Louisville Courier-Journal,* and was a 1989 finalist for the Pulitzer Prize in news photography. A three-time Kentucky Newspaper Photographer of the Year, he was awarded an Eclipse Award for the best horse racing photograph of the year. His works regularly for *Sports Illustrated, Time, Newsweek, The New York Times Magazine, Fortune, Southern Living* and *People,* among others. Ben was one of 80 photographers who participated in the "Day in the

Life of the NHL" book project, where one of his photographs was chosen for the cover. On the staff of the *National Sports Daily,* he shot Super Bowls, World Series, NBA Finals and the top horse and auto races around the country. Ben placed more photographs in *Bryant-Denny Saturday* than any other photographer.

TCI PRESIDENT & CEO
LINDA F. HIGGISON

Mrs. Higgison, founder and President, is a recognized leader in the field of destination and special event management. Her insights and business focus have contributed significantly to the development of a one-time cottage industry into a serious business endeavor. As such, destination management services are valued by corporate and association clients as vital to the success of their marketing strategies. For eight years, she served on the Board of Directors of THE NETWORK, a nationwide consortium of leading destination management firms, and served as President in 1989. During her tenure, she wrote the first definitive statement and business analysis of the highly fragmented $300-million destination management specialty, and its role within the hospitality industry. Mrs. Higgison was a 1996 Finalist in Ernst & Young's Washington, DC Entrepreneur of the Year Award. This award was established to honor and recognize entrepreneurs who have demonstrated excellence and extraordinary success in areas of financial performance, innovation and personal commitment to their business and communities.

Mrs. Higgison is an active member of several community-, education- and industry-related organizations. She serves on the Greater Washington Board of Trade, the Washington, Baltimore, Charlotte and Birmingham Convention and Visitors Associations, and the Advisory Board of the Charlotte Chamber of Commerce. She has also served on the Greater Washington Initiative. Besides sitting on the faculty of the George Washington University School of Business' Sport and Event Marketing Forum, she has been a guest lecturer and has served on the Board of Advisors. Mrs. Higgison is on the steering committee of the University of Alabama's College of Education, and on the board of the National Foundation for Women Legislators. She is a member of the Professional Convention Management Association, and is a contributing editor for *Convention South* magazine. Through company-sponsored programs, she has been an active fund-raiser for historic properties, the Washington Cathedral, the Friends of the First Ladies Foundation and Tudor Place where she also served as a Trustee.

PROJECT MARKETING & SPONSORSHIP
THE TCI COMPANIES

The TCI Companies is a full-service organization that markets and implements a broad spectrum of meetings, special events and sponsorship programs for corporations, trade associations and non-profit organizations. The TCI Companies, formerly The Capital Informer, was founded in 1977 by Linda Higgison as a Washington, DC-based destination management company. In 1996, TCI reorganized into four in-house operating divisions to position itself for national expansion and internal growth. This innovative company has managed over 50,000 events and meetings for an estimated 5,000 clients across the country. The TCI headquarters is located in Washington, DC. TCI has recently opened an office in Charlotte, North Carolina, which specializes in sports-related events, promotions and sponsorships.

The various divisions of The TCI Companies include The Capital Informer, a pioneer and recognized leader in meeting and event management; TCI Marketing, which designs and executes destination and event marketing and sponsorship programs; Transportation Concepts International, which plans and manages the transportation needs of clients; and

Team Concepts International, which provides sports-related and hands-on training programs. It also plans and manages sponsored sports events for corporations and trade associations. The TCI Companies clients include IBM, American Express, National Association of Manufacturers, Xerox, American Bankers Association, Independent Bankers Association of America, Mortgage Bankers Association and Mobil Oil. Recent clients include the National Quarterback Awards Program, The Bronko Nagurski Trophy Award, Britain's 1998 Whitbread Round the World Sailing Race, Kraft Foods, Serento Laboratories, American Urological Association, PROMAX and NatWest Marketing (National Westminister Bank).

The TCI Companies is a globally recognized advocate in the $82-billion hospitality industry and is known for creating and promoting new services which are helping to change the way meetings, events and conventions are run and financed.

PHOTOGRAPHER
ANNIE GRIFFITHS BELT

Annie is a *National Geographic* contract photographer, born and raised in Minneapolis. Her professional career began while she was still attending the University of Minnesota when she worked as a staff photographer for the *Minnesota Daily.* After graduating with a Bachelor of Arts in 1976, she joined the staff of the award-winning *Worthington Daily Globe* in southern Minnesota. She began assignment work for the National Geographic Society in 1978. Since then, she has worked on dozens of magazine and book projects for the Society, including *National Geographic* magazine stories on Baja California, Israel's Galilee, Britain's Pennine Way, Vancouver, England's Lake District and Jerusalem. She is currently working on stories for *National Geographic* in the Middle East, Central America and the United States. Her photographs have been exhibited in New York, Washington, Moscow and Tokyo. She has received awards from the National Press Photography Association, the Associated Press, the National Organization of Women and the White House News Photographers Association. Last summer, Annie appeared in a public television documentary about her work.

PHOTOGRAPHER
NICOLE BENGIVENO

Nicole is a freelance photographer based in New York City and associated with Matrix International Agency. She receives assignments for numerous publications and magazines, especially *US News and World Report.* She was a staff photographer for the *San Francisco Examiner* from 1979-1986 and for the *New York Daily News* from 1986-1994. Since 1980 she has participated in 12 "Day in the Life" book projects. She was named San Francisco Bay Area Photographer of the Year and Eugene Smith Award finalist for work with AIDS. She won first place awards from the New York Associated Press for her coverage in the Soviet Union.

PHOTOGRAPHER - JIM GENSHEIMER

Jim is a photojournalist for the *San Jose Mercury News.* Two-time California Photographer of the Year, he is a graduate of Western Kentucky University, and former intern at the *National Geographic.* Before moving to California in 1984, Jim worked at his hometown paper, *The Louisville Courier-Journal.* In 1995, he was the first American newspaper photojournalist to visit North Korea. Other international assignments include trips to Vietnam and Thailand to document the plight of Vietnamese boat people, and to Norway to photograph the 1994 Winter Olympics. He has worked on several book projects including *A Day in the Life of California, In Pursuit of Ideas, Once Upon a Dream* and *24 Hours in Cyberspace.*

PHOTOGRAPHER - LYNN JOHNSON

Lynn Johnson is known for sensitive, documentary work in both color and black & white, producing photo essays for such magazines as *National Geographic, Life, Sports Illustrated, Fortune, Forbes, Newsweek, The New York Times Magazine* and *Smithsonian*. In search of pictures, Lynn has climbed the radio antennae atop Chicago's Hancock Tower, and eaten rats with Vietcong guerrillas. She has traveled from the Antarctic to Tibet and done in-depth portraits of such celebrities as Mikhail Baryshnikov, Stevie Wonder, Michael Douglas, Gloria Estefan, Mr. Rogers, and the entire Supreme Court. Lynn earned a B.A. in Photographic Illustration and Photojournalism at the Rochester Institute of Technology in 1975. She was a staff photographer at *The Pittsburgh Press* before joining New York's Black Star photo agency in 1984. Now with Aurora, she has received many awards including seven Golden Quills for Photojournalism, four World Press Photography Awards, the Robert F. Kennedy Journalism Award and Picture of the Year Award from the National Press Photographer Association at the University of Missouri School of Journalism.

PHOTOGRAPHER - ART MERIPOL

Art is the Senior Photographer for Travel at *Southern Living* magazine. He began his career in Arkansas, working at newspapers there and in Texas, covering the Dallas Cowboys and Houston Oilers on a regular basis. At the *Arkansas Gazette,* he was a leading photographer covering Southwest Conference football and basketball. His awards include first in News in Texas Associated Press, and first in News, Sports and second in Features in Texas UPI contests. He also won in the Arkansas AP and UPI contests and earned several "Best of Gannett" awards. Art's work has been included twice in University of Missouri's "Best of Photo Journalism" Pictures of the Year exhibit. Art's work also appears in *Cooking Light, Southern Accents, Vacations* and *Progressive Farmer* magazine. Art also participated in *Bryant-Denny Saturday.*

PHOTOGRAPHER - RICK RICKMAN

Rick won the Pulitzer Prize for News Photography in 1985, and was named National Sports Photographer of the Year in 1995. Rick also photographed the 1996 Centennial Olympic Games in Atlanta, shooting for *Newsweek*. He has been a finalist in the W. Eugene Smith Memorial Grant, and has received numerous awards in the Picture of the Year competition. He is a graduate of New Mexico State and has had photos appear in *National Geographic, Life, Time, Geo, People* and *Audubon*. Rick has also photographed for major corporations including Allstate, Magnavox, AT&T, Phillip Morris and John Deere. His work has been exhibited internationally as part of traveling shows in the Smithsonian Museum in the United States, and as major cultural expos in Germany and Japan. He has been featured on PBS and has lectured to photography workshops and corporate seminars. He has photographed for *In Pursuit of Ideas* and four "Day in the Life" books as well as other large subject books on Christmas, the Jewish lifestyle, baseball and healing.

PHOTOGRAPHER - DAVID ROARK

A Florida native, David is the Supervisor of Photographic Creative for Attractions Marketing at the Walt Disney World Resort. He received his first professional photography assignment when he was 17. He has been with the Walt Disney Company for 15 years, photographing not only in Florida, but in Disney theme parks in Tokyo and France, as well as Disneyland in California. He is responsible for the production of advertising photography for the Walt Disney World Resort, and his photographs have appeared in major magazines worldwide. He has received more than 20 Addy awards for advertising photography. David shot special portraits of "Fans" for *Bryant-Denny Saturday.*

PHOTOGRAPHER - JOEL SARTORE

Joel is Oklahoma-born and Nebraska-bred. A contract photographer with *National Geographic,* he is considered one of the best young photographers in the country today. He graduated from the University of Nebraska in 1985 with a BA in Journalism and worked as a staff photographer with the *Wichita Eagle,* where he became director of photography for the paper in 1990. Joel was the winner of the Award of Excellence, Magazine Photographer of the Year category in the 1992 Picture of the Year competition. He has won individual "Picture of the Year" awards in the past five years, and was 1986 Photographer of the Year in the National Press Photographers Association, Region 7. Joel produced some of the most memorable images for *Bryant-Denny Saturday.*

PHOTOGRAPHER - SCOTT WISEMAN

Scott is a staff photographer for the *Palm Beach Post.* Before joining the *Post*, he worked at the *Nashville Banner* and *The San Bernardino Sun* (California). He has won first place in the William Randolph Hearst Photojournalism Championship competition. He has also won numerous photographic awards from the National Press Photographers Association (NPPA), the Pictures of the Year competition, Atlanta Seminar on Photojournalism, NPPA Monthly National Clip Contests, The Society of Newspaper Design, Florida Society of Newspaper Editors and the Southern Shortcourse on Photography, among others. At the *Palm Beach Post,* Scott has covered the Miami Dolphins, Florida Marlins, Florida Panthers, Miami Heat, Florida Gators, Florida State Seminoles and Miami Hurricanes.

CAROLINA PANTHERS
TEAM PHOTOGRAPHER
SCOTT CUNNINGHAM

Scott has been the Panthers' Team Photographer since their very first exhibition game in 1995. An experienced sports photographer, the Roanoke, Va. native shot Virginia Tech basketball and football while still in high school, then moved to Georgia to study at the Art Institute of Atlanta. He began shooting for the Atlanta Braves, Flames and Hawks, becoming the Hawks team photographer in 1979. In 1980, he was named the Atlanta Falcons official photographer, and in 1988 was selected the Washington Redskins official photographer. Scott has hundreds of sports magazine covers to his credit. He is currently a contract photographer for the National Basketball Association, shooting more than 100 games in each of the last three years. In 1988, Scott toured the former Soviet Union with the Atlanta Hawks on assignment for *Sports Illustrated* shooting games at arenas in Moscow; Vilnius, Lithuania; and Tbilisi, Soviet Georgia. In 1987, he spent the entire NASCAR season documenting Richard Petty's activities on and off the track, producing a very successful photo book, *The World of King Richard.* Just prior to joining the *Carolina Panthers Sunday* staff, Scott finished producing and editing the *Official History of the Washington Redskins.*

RICHARDSON FAMILY PHOTOGRAPHER
LES DUGGINS

Les began his career with the *Herald-Journal* newspaper as their primary sports photographer in 1973. He opened his own photography studio in 1980. In 1990, Les had an opportunity to work for Jerry Richardson and Flagstar as manager of Flagstar Creative Services Photography department. In 1994, Les began photographing events for the Carolina Panthers and in 1995 he was officially named as one of the team photographers. Les has studied with world-renowned photographers Al Gilbert, Frank Cricchio and Mitch Kezar of Winona International School of Professional Photography. Les' work has appeared in *Time, Beckett's, Sports Image, Axel Springer* and *Kickoff '96* magazines as well as other publications.

TCI COMPANIES, TEAM CONCEPTS
INTERNATONAL DIRECTOR
RON PETERSON

Ron, a veteran of corporate and sports marketing, is the Director of Team Concepts International and head of The TCI Companies' Charlotte office. Before joining TCI, he was the executive director of the Charlotte Organizing Committee for the U.S. Olympic Team Trials-Cycling, the Charlotte Touchdown Club, and the coordinator of Charlotte's ACC Men's Basketball tournament bid for 1999-2001. He was previously a sales and marketing executive for Coca-Cola USA. Prior to that, he was an

Fred Sisson, Nikon Professional Services, and Laurie Bernard, Eastman Kodak Professional Imaging Markets Manager.

account supervisor at The Richards Group, a full-service advertising agency, where he directed the multi-million dollar Whataburger account, arranging sponsorships and promotions for various professional, collegiate and high school sports teams, and coordinated the use of athletes as corporate spokespersons. He was published in *The Journal of Advertising Research*. Ron earned a Bachelor of Science in Marketing from the University of Texas at Austin, and obtained his Master of Business Administration from Southern Methodist University.

SHOOT PRODUCER - NINA SABO

Nina has produced studio and location photography shoots for clients such as Nikon and *Life* magazine. For Nikon, Nina coordinated the extensive planning of photo shoots for the N90s, SB26 and F5 product lines. For these productions, she did location scouting, made travel arrangements, negotiated contracts with modeling agencies, and worked with stylists and camera crews, all the while overseeing production budgets for these complex shoots. For *Life,* she produced a series of shots which involved Michelle Pfeiffer wearing the Smithsonian Institute's entire multi-million dollar national gem collection. Most recently for *Life,* she produced a portfolio of world-famous Olympic athletes for photojournalist Joe McNally. This involved coordinating the busy schedules of the athletes, securing shoot locations all over the United States and being ready for the unexpected. Nina's agenda also includes her own photography work involving assignments for design firms, advertising clients and magazines. She currently resides in Westchester County, New York.

CHIEF PHOTOGRAPHY ASSISTANT
MARK ASHMAN

Mark is currently a freelance photographer working in Orlando, Florida. Born in Lincoln, Nebraska, Mark attended the University of Nebraska at Kearney where he graduated with a degree in advertising and journalism with an emphasis on photography. He then furthered his education at the Southeast Center for Photo/Graphic Studies in Daytona Beach, Florida. He has won awards from the Nebraska Press Association for best sports action photo, the Nebraska Press Photographers Association first place in general news photo and second in both feature photo and general news photo. His photographs have appeared in *USA Today, The Disney Magazine, Barbie* magazine, and *Parade*. Mark has worked as a photographer's assistant for *Sports Illustrated, People, The New York Times Magazine* and others. He has also worked on shoots for such corporations as Kodak, AT&T and AAA publications. He also served as President of the Photographic Society during his work at the Southeast Museum of Photography in Daytona Beach.

ADMINISTRATIVE MANAGER
LAREE BROWN

Laree is a Muscle Shoals, Alabama native who has worked with photography and photographers for nearly five years. As a shoot coordinator and talent manager, she has prepared and scouted photo locations, assigned work, logged film and supervised quality control, as well as assisting with shoots. She has worked events such as the National Press Photographers annual convention, the NBA All Star Weekend, the *Aladdin* movie premiere for Walt Disney Pictures, the Splash Mountain grand opening at Walt Disney World Magic Kingdom, the Planet Hollywood groundbreaking in Orlando, The Academy of Television Arts and Sciences Hall of Fame Induction and gala at the Disney-MGM Studios in Florida, and numerous *Southern Living* photo shoots. She currently resides in Birmingham, Alabama.

FACILITIES & EQUIPMENT MANAGER
JERRY BROWN

Jerry is an Alabama native, former athlete and private business owner who has been involved with sports all his life. He played tight end for the legendary Coach Paul "Bear" Bryant at the University of Alabama from 1972-1977, lettering two years, and was a member of the 1973 National Champion Crimson Tide team. After receiving his Bachelor of Science in both Real Estate Finance and Business Education, Jerry worked for banks and savings and loan institutions in Central Alabama, before starting his own businesses, concentrating on sporting goods and personal services. He has been a leading member of the Alabama State High School Athletic Association, officiating for 19 years throughout the state and serving as a member of the local board of directors in Tuscaloosa. Jerry also assisted with the business organization and shooting preparation for *Bryant-Denny Saturday*.

COORDINATOR - CHRISTINA FETTERS

Christina is as comfortable in front of the camera as she is behind the scenes. Her professional work includes feature films, television specials and series, broadcast commercials, print commercials, live shows and theater work. The Cambridge, Ohio native began her career as a scholarship recipient training and performing with the Pittsburgh Ballet Theatre. The transition into film work took place in Florida performing in a Rich Little commercial. She toured overseas with Julio Iglesias in 1988, and quickly achieved a reputation for hard work. Her performances as a theme park dancer then led to roles as a stunt-woman for the syndicated series *Thunder in Paradise*. Other roles followed in *SeaQuest, Fortune Hunter, Pointman, Tarzan* the series, *Unsolved Mysteries* and *Savannah*. Her feature films include *Fair Game, Shadow Conspiracy, Marvin's Room* and *Fled* among others. Christina has worked coordinating live action production for Aqua Leisure, and still photography shoots for Eddie Adams. She currently resides in Orlando.

COORDINATOR - CECE WILCK

CeCe was born in Los Angeles, where she had a successful career as a talent agent representing some of America's top models and celebrities such as Chynna Phillips, Uma Thurman and Tia Carrera. In 1991, she joined Summer Place Productions, a leading Los Angeles production company, where as a production manager she supervised all facets of pre- and post-production, coordinated location shoots and hired crew and talent. Some of her projects included Alice Cooper music videos and a *Tribute to Marvin Gaye*. She was promoted to Associate Producer where her varied work included the children's video *Greg and Steve's Musical Adventures*, which won the Parents Choice Award as Best Children's Video of 1992. She currently resides in Orlando, Florida, where she is a successful commercial actress appearing in commercials for Sprint, *ABC's Monday Night Football*, Martini & Rossi, Nordic Track and Central Florida theme parks.

BOOK DESIGNER - BEN BURFORD

Ben is founder and owner of DynaType, Inc. in Birmingham, Alabama. The company has produced numerous Addy Award-winning brochures, pamphlets, and advertising campaigns for print and broadcast media. Ben is non-traditional in all aspects of his life, and will do just about anything for money, including long-term stints as a professional actor and vocalist.

PRINT COORDINATOR - GLENN PETRY

Glenn is originally from Indianapolis, Indiana. He has worked in the Graphic Arts industry in Orlando, Florida, for the past twelve years. Glenn is nationally recognized with more than 46-years of experience in all phases of printing. He has judged The Printing Industry of Texas competition for the past eight years, and the Printing Industry of America International competition for the past four years.

COLOR SEPARATIONS & PAGE ASSEMBLY

Ropkey Graphics, Indianapolis, Indiana

PRINTING

White Arts Press, Indianapolis, Indiana

EDITOR'S NOTE

Special thanks to the Carolina Panthers organization for their assistance in producing this book. Exceptional assistance was provided by the Richardson family, Charlie Dayton, Lex Sant and Tom Fellows.

Carolina Panthers Sunday Student Assistant Staff

Photographer
MARK ASHMAN